GRADES 1-2

WORDS IN CONTEXT
ANIMALS

CYNTHIA WILLIAMSON

New York • Toronto • London
Auckland • Sydney • New Delhi • Hong Kong

Photos ©: National Geographic Creative: 48 (Paul Nicklen); Shutterstock: cover left (Eric Isselee), cover top right (Kuttelvaserova Stuchelova), cover bottom right (Sergei Mironenko), 9 (Cassiohabib), 12 (Elena_sg80), 15 (Yoshinori), 21 (Sergey Uryadnikov), 24 (graja), 27 (FJAH), 33 (Ondrej Prosicky), 36 (Viktor Hejna), 39 (Tom Reichner), 45 (FloridaStock), 54 (Dreamnord), 57 (Dennis W Donohue), 60 (teekayu), 65 (atm2003), 66 (Dennis W Donohue), 69 (Kristof Kovacs), 72 (shameer pk), 78 (Vasilyev Alexandr), 81 (Andrzej Kubik), 84 (Vinnikava Viktoryia), 90 (xkunclova), 93 (Meet Poddar), 96 (Wittawat Pawpraseart), 101 (Richard Peterson), 102 (Liz Miller), 105 (miroslav chytil), 108 (Pim Leijen), 113 left (MAZM MAZM), 113 right (Alexey Kabanov), 114 (Jan Bures), 117 (Worraket).

Editor: Maria L. Chang
Cover design: Tannaz Fassihi
Interior design: Michelle H. Kim

Scholastic Inc., 557 Broadway, New York, NY 10012
ISBN: 978-1-338-28563-5
Copyright © 2020 by Cynthia Williamson
All rights reserved.
Printed in the U.S.A.
First printing, January 2020.

1 2 3 4 5 6 7 8 9 10   40   25 24 23 22 21 20

Table of Contents

INTRODUCTION

In school and in life, there is great value in having a rich vocabulary. Knowing the meaning and correct usage of many words allows us to express our own ideas and understand those of others. And it is essential for reading comprehension.

Words in Context: Animals uses a contextual approach—as well as high-interest subject matter—to help children build a rich and varied vocabulary. First, they listen as you read aloud a text passage with contextual clues, and they guess the meaning of boldface words. Then, they study the proper definitions, and they complete sentences using the vocabulary words. Next, children show what they've learned by composing their own sentences using the words. Research shows that this approach is far more effective than just memorizing definitions (Nash & Snowling, 2006)—and it's clearly more engaging to children!

Focusing on the theme of animals of the world, this book provides ten months of comprehensive vocabulary instruction. Most months (except for December and June) include materials for three weeks of instruction, with three vocabulary sheets per week—two for classroom instruction and one quiz to demonstrate independent application of skills.

Words in Context: Animals addresses a wide range of core literacy standards, including:

- **CCSS.ELA–LITERACY.L.1.4 and 2.4:** Determine or clarify the meaning of unknown and multiple-meaning words and phrases based on grade-appropriate reading and context, choosing flexibly from an array of strategies.

- **CCSS.ELA–LITERACY.L.1.4.A and 2.4.A:** Use sentence-level context as a clue to the meaning of a word or phrase.

The fourth week of each month is devoted to cumulative review for a monthly assessment. (Since most districts have a shorter schedule in December and June, we offer only two weeks of vocabulary instruction and a third week for review and assessment.) The book also includes various bonus tasks, as well as monthly enrichment activities.

PROCEDURE FOR WEEKLY INSTRUCTION

Below is a suggested instructional routine for teaching vocabulary with this book.

MONDAY

Distribute the corresponding vocabulary sheets A and B.

Begin with sheet A. Project the sheet and read the paragraph aloud.* Then, reread the sentences in which the vocabulary words appear. (As the school year progresses and students' fluency increases, you may choose to call on individual children to read aloud to the class.) Encourage children to guess the meaning of each word by considering the context in which it appears. Guide your discussion by asking questions such as:

• *Have you ever seen this word in print before? Have you heard it spoken?*

• *Does the word describe something? Is it an action—something you can do?*

Record children's guesses on the whiteboard. Then, have them refer to the list to fill in their guesses on sheet A. Next, turn to sheet B and read the correct definitions. Compare children's guesses to the actual definitions. Finally, read and complete the given sentences as a class.

TUESDAY

Review the definitions of the three vocabulary words orally. With the class, compose sentences using these words.

WEDNESDAY

Copy and distribute vocabulary sheet C and give children 15 to 20 minutes to complete it independently or with minimal support. Collect and correct. To monitor progress on a monthly basis, average children's performance on these sheets.

THURSDAY

Review vocabulary sheet C.

FRIDAY

Allow children to share their work on the bonus tasks with the class.

Devote the last week of every month to reviewing the six or nine vocabulary words studied over the past three weeks, completing the cumulative assessment, and engaging in the enrichment activity.

NOTE: Some of the text passages use vocabulary words from preceding weeks. Challenge children to identify such words and review the definitions. Do the same if you happen to come across any of the words in other reading materials. Research shows that we need to see, read, and use a word multiple times before it is encoded in our long-term memory. How many times? That depends on each individual child's literacy skills. This could range from as few as four times for your top students to as many as 40 times for your English language learners.

---

* While this worksheet and the cumulative assessment are designed to demonstrate independent application of skills, it is unlikely that first graders will be able to do so initially. Use your professional judgment to provide each child with the support he or she needs. Paraprofessional support with your special-education students as well as English language learners would be invaluable as you work toward the goal of independent application of skills. I recommend that you read aloud the paragraph to your class before children attempt to complete the vocabulary sheet and the assessment on their own.

OVERALL THEME:
Animals of the World

SEPTEMBER: Sea Life

OCTOBER: Hibernating Animals

NOVEMBER: Birds

DECEMBER: Arctic Animals

JANUARY: Apes and Monkeys

FEBRUARY: Wild Cats

MARCH: Farm Animals

APRIL: Pets

MAY: Wild Dogs

JUNE: Reptiles

NOTE: As the school year progresses, it is likely that some children will be able to read the paragraphs on their own, either aloud or silently. You may opt to have children follow along as you reread each passage aloud. This is not only a research-based strategy for building fluency, but the inflection of your voice can communicate many valuable clues as to the meaning of the words.

ENRICHMENT ACTIVITIES AND BONUS TASKS

Each month concludes with an enrichment activity that supports multisensory learning for children of all abilities. If possible, complete these activities as a class. If not, have children do them at home with their families.

Bonus tasks are included on vocabulary sheets B and C. Many of the tasks on sheet B give children the opportunity for reflective learning—thinking about what they have learned and relating it to their own lives. A growing body of research suggests that reflection promotes meaningful, lasting learning and helps children feel in control of their own progress. An example of a reflective learning activity is when children are asked to "make a list of foods you most like to feast upon." (Of course, *feast* is one of the week's vocabulary words.)

Other tasks help facilitate quick word retrieval, which is important because children often have a gap between the words they understand (receptive vocabulary) and the words they can remember and use in daily life (expressive vocabulary).

While these bonus tasks will keep your "fast finishers" busy as you work with children who need additional support, they should never be considered "busy work." Make sure all children have adequate time to complete them.

Reference: Nash, H., & Snowling, M. (2006). Teaching new words to children with poor existing vocabulary knowledge: A controlled evaluation of the definition and context methods. *International Journal of Language & Communication Disorders*, 41(3), 335–354.

Jellyfish

Jellyfish float in oceans all over the world. Some jellyfish are large and colorful. Others are small and **clear**. They look like umbrellas floating on the water **surface**. They have dozens of long arms, called *tentacles*. Jellyfish use their tentacles to get food. Don't worry! Most jellyfish eat tiny sea plants and animals. You should still **avoid** jellyfish anyway. Their tentacles can sting. Ouch!

Reread the sentences where you see these words. What do you think each word means?

clear: _____

surface: _____

avoid: _____

Name: _____   Date: _____

Read what each word means.
Then fill in each blank with the correct word.

> **clear:** easy to see through
>
> **surface:** the top or outside part of something
>
> **avoid:** to stay away from

1. On a summer day, the lake is calm and _____.

2. It's not always easy to _____ trouble.

3. Dry, dusty soil covers the _____ of the moon.

BONUS **Complete the following sentences.**

- I always try to **avoid** _____.

- But I never **avoid** _____.

Name: _____   Date: _____

Draw a line to match each word with its meaning.

clear   • to stay away from

surface   • easy to see through

avoid   • the top or outside part
                                     of something

Write a sentence using one of the vocabulary words.
(Your sentence should begin with a capital letter
and end with a period.)

_____

_____

BONUS Is it true that a jellyfish's arms are called *tentacles*?
(Check one.)

☐ Yes   ☐ No

Name: _____ Date: _____

Seahorses

Believe it or not, seahorses are actually fish! These tiny fish look **odd**. They have long snouts and long tails. They swim in warm, **shallow** waters. Sometimes, two seahorses swim together with their tails linked. They can also wrap their tails around sea grasses. That keeps the waves from carrying them out to the deep sea. Seahorses can change their colors. This helps them hide from enemies. Some seahorses have sharp spines. It is best not to touch seahorses. Don't you **agree**?

Reread the sentences where you see these words. What do you think each word means?

odd: _____

shallow: _____

agree: _____

Read what each word means.
Then fill in each blank with the correct word.

> **odd:** strange; weird
>
> **shallow:** not deep
>
> **agree:** to think the same way

1. Don't you _____ that birthday parties
   are lots of fun?

2. My little brother swims in the _____ end
   of the pool.

3. Wouldn't it be _____ if it snowed in the
   middle of summer?

BONUS **Draw a picture of something you find odd.**

Draw a line to match each word with its meaning.

odd   • not deep

shallow   • to think the same way

agree   • strange; weird

Write a sentence using one of the vocabulary words.
(Your sentence should begin with a capital letter
and end with a period.)

_____

_____

BONUS **Is it true that seahorses can change their colors?**
(Check one.)

☐ Yes   ☐ No

     Words in Context: Animals © Cynthia Williamson, Scholastic Inc.

Name: _____ Date: _____

Sharks

Do sharks make you **shiver** with fear? If so, you are not alone. Many people think sharks are scary. Sharks have rows of sharp teeth in their mouths. Their dark, round eyes never blink.

Sharks swim at a **steady** pace. They **prowl** the ocean to hunt for fish. But they do not often attack humans.

There are more than 400 different kinds of sharks. One of the largest is the gentle, harmless basking shark. It swims near the surface of warm ocean waters. This shark eats only very small sea animals and plants.

Reread the sentences where you see these words. What do you think each word means?

shiver: _____

steady: _____

prowl: _____

Read what each word means.
Then fill in each blank with the correct word.

> **shiver:** to shake with cold or fear
>
> **steady:** not changing
>
> **prowl:** to move around in a sneaky way

1. Some cats _____ at night, looking for a meal.

2. The cold wind made Mayna _____.

3. A _____ stream of water came out of the fire hydrant.

BONUS **Draw a picture of something that might make you shiver.**

Words in Context: Animals © Cynthia Williamson, Scholastic Inc.

Name: _____   Date: _____

Draw a line to match each word with its meaning.

shiver   • not changing

prowl   • to shake with cold or fear

steady   • to move around in a sneaky way

Write a sentence using one of the vocabulary words.
(Your sentence should begin with a capital letter
and end with a period.)

_____

_____

BONUS **Is it true that the basking shark eats other sharks?**
(Check one.)

☐ **Yes**   ☐ **No**

Cumulative Review

Review the meaning of each vocabulary word below.

agree: to think the same way

avoid: to stay away from

clear: easy to see through

odd: strange; weird

prowl: to move around in a sneaky way

shallow: not deep

shiver: to shake with cold or fear

steady: not changing

surface: the top or outside part of something

Name: _____ Date: _____

1. Write the meaning of each word. (25 points each)

agree: _____

surface: _____

2. Pick one of the words below.
   Write a sentence using that word. (50 points)

steady	shallow	clear	prowl

_____

_____

BONUS **Is it true that some seahorses swim together with their tails linked?** (+5 points)

☐ Yes   ☐ No

Jellyfish in a Bottle

Have students make little jellyfish that float in a bottle.

YOU'LL NEED

- plastic wrap
- small rubber bands or lengths of thread
- scissors
- clear plastic soda or water bottles* (one for each child)
- water
- blue and green food coloring

* Ask children to bring in a clean bottle from home. Have extras on hand for those who don't have one.

TO DO

1 Give each child a 6-inch square of plastic wrap and a rubber band or length of thread.

2 Show children how to scrunch up the plastic wrap to form a little head and secure it with a tiny rubber band or tie it with thread.

3 To create their jellyfish's "tentacles," have children cut the plastic beneath the head into strips. Tell them to be careful not to cut the strips off. They'll want to keep the tentacles attached to the head.

4 Give each child a plastic bottle filled three-quarters of the way with water. Have them add a drop of blue and/or green food coloring until the water is the color of the sea. (You may want to enlist adult volunteers to help with this.)

5 Have children put their "jellyfish" into the colored water. Cap the bottle tightly and shake. They'll see the jellyfish drift, flutter, and billow in the bottle, much like they do in the ocean.

TAKE IT FURTHER

If possible, schedule time for your students to visit pre-K and kindergarten classes to show the younger children their jellyfish and to share what they've learned about these sea animals.

Words in Context: Animals © Cynthia Williamson, Scholastic Inc.

Name: _____   Date: _____

Bears

Did you know that some animals sleep all winter long? This is called *hibernating*. Animals hibernate to stay warm when the weather is cold. Sleeping also helps them save energy when food is **scarce**.

Bears hibernate. In the fall, these **massive** animals eat as much as they can. Then they look for **cozy** dens. They move in for the winter. Some bears sleep for as long as seven months. Bears that live in warmer places don't sleep as long.

**Reread the sentences where you see these words.
What do you think each word means?**

scarce: _____

massive: _____

cozy: _____

Note: Some experts say bears are not true hibernators. Even though bears can sleep for several months without getting up to eat, drink, or relieve themselves, they can wake up quickly if there is danger.

Name: _____   Date: _____

Read what each word means.
Then fill in each blank with the correct word.

> **scarce:** hard to find
>
> **massive:** very large and heavy
>
> **cozy:** warm and comfortable

1. Water is _____ in the desert.

2. Our house is small but _____.

3. My tiny puppy might grow up to be a _____ dog.

BONUS **Draw a picture of something that is cozy.**

Words in Context: Animals © Cynthia Williamson, Scholastic Inc.

Name: _____   Date: _____

Draw a line to match each word with its meaning.

scarce   • very large and heavy

massive   • warm and comfortable

cozy   • hard to find

Write a sentence using one of the vocabulary words.
(Your sentence should begin with a capital letter
and end with a period.)

_____

_____

BONUS **Is it true that bears can sleep for as long as seven
months?** (Check one.)

☐ Yes   ☐ No

Name: _____ Date: _____

Ladybugs

In the summer, ladybugs help our gardens grow. They eat small bugs that are **harmful** to plants.

As the weather gets colder, these red-and-black insects start looking for a place to hibernate. Large groups of ladybugs will **huddle** together under logs or inside trees. This helps them keep warm. They sleep the winter away. Some may move into a house's cozy corners. But most people **prefer** that ladybugs stay outdoors.

**Reread the sentences where you see these words.
What do you think each word means?**

harmful: _____

huddle: _____

prefer: _____

Words in Context: Animals © Cynthia Williamson, Scholastic Inc.

Name: _____ Date: _____

Read what each word means.
Then fill in each blank with the correct word.

> **harmful:** can hurt or cause damage
>
> **huddle:** to come close together in a tight group
>
> **prefer:** to like one thing better than another

1. I _____ funny movies to scary ones.

2. The kittens like to _____ near their mother.

3. _____ germs can make you sick.

BONUS **Complete the following sentence:**

I prefer _____

instead of _____.

Draw a line to match each word with its meaning.

harmful   • to come close together
                                             in a tight group

prefer   • can hurt or cause damage

huddle   • to like one thing better
                                             than another

Write a sentence using one of the vocabulary words.
(Your sentence should begin with a capital letter
and end with a period.)

_____

_____

BONUS **Is it true that ladybugs are harmful to our gardens?**
(Check one.)

☐ Yes   ☐ No

Words in Context: Animals © Cynthia Williamson, Scholastic Inc.

Name: _____   Date: _____

Bats

Bats **soar** high in the sky. But they are not birds. They are *mammals*— warm-blooded animals that feed their young with milk.

Bats like to huddle in cozy, dark places. They sleep all winter. A bat may also hibernate in the attic of a house. This may make people who live in the house **nervous**. But most bats are harmless. Many **feast** only on insects.

There are more than 1,000 different kinds of bats. The largest kind of bat is called a flying fox. The smallest is the bumblebee bat.

**Reread the sentences where you see these words.
What do you think each word means?**

soar: _____

nervous: _____

feast: _____

Read what each word means.
Then fill in each blank with the correct word.

> **soar:** to fly very high
>
> **nervous:** feeling worried or afraid
>
> **feast:** to eat a lot of something

1. I felt _____ on the first day of school.

2. Wouldn't it be fun to _____ in the sky like a bird?

3. On my birthday, I will _____ on ice cream.

BONUS **Make a list of the three foods you most like to feast on.**

- _____

- _____

- _____

Name: _____   Date: _____

Draw a line to match each word with its meaning.

nervous   • to fly very high

soar   • feeling worried or afraid

feast   • to eat a lot of something

Write a sentence using one of the vocabulary words.
(Your sentence should begin with a capital letter
and end with a period.)

_____

_____

BONUS **Is it true that the smallest type of bat is called a flying fox?** (Check one.)

☐ Yes   ☐ No

Cumulative Review

Review the meaning of each vocabulary word below.

cozy: warm and comfortable

feast: to eat a lot of something

harmful: can hurt or cause damage

huddle: to come close together in a tight group

massive: very large and heavy

nervous: feeling worried or afraid

prefer: to like one thing better than another

scarce: hard to find

soar: to fly very high

Name: _____   Date: _____

1. Write the meaning of each word. (25 points each)

massive: _____

soar: _____

2. Pick one of the words below.
   Write a sentence using that word. (50 points)

| nervous | huddle | scarce | harmful |

_____

_____

BONUS **Is it true that bats are mammals?** (+5 points)

☐ Yes   ☐ No

Bear in a Cave

**Children will enjoy creating their own stuffed bear and making a cozy home for it.
Time frame:** 2 days

YOU'LL NEED

- brown construction paper
- scissors
- markers or crayons
- stapler
- shredded paper
- shoeboxes, one for each child*
- pebbles, twigs, cotton balls
- glue

* Ask children to bring in a shoebox from home. Have extras on hand for those who don't have one.

TO DO

1 Trace a simple outline of a bear on brown construction paper. Make two for each child—front and back.

2 Have children cut out the bear (great for building fine-motor skills) and draw a face on the front.

3 Staple a back onto the bear, leaving the top unstapled. Have children carefully stuff the bear with shredded paper through the top. Then staple the bear closed.

4 Ask children to bring a shoebox, as well as a collection of pebbles and twigs, to school for the next part of this craft activity.

5 On another day, have children create a cave for their bear using the shoebox, twigs, and pebbles. Have them use cotton balls to simulate snow on top of the cave. Use regular glue or low-heat glue guns to attach the pebbles, twigs, and cotton balls to the top of the box. (If you choose to use glue guns, you may want to invite parent volunteers to assist.)

6 Have children use crayons or markers to draw the interior of the cave. Suggest they add a group of hibernating ladybugs or bats, too. Finally, have them place their hibernating bear inside the cave.

Name: _____   Date: _____

Hummingbirds

Hummingbirds are the smallest birds in the world. These **dainty** birds are about the size of a dragonfly. Hummingbirds are the only kind of bird that can fly backwards. They can also fly for many, many miles. They **hover** in the air as they

suck sweet juice from flowers. Sometimes they feast on insects, too.

There are about 300 different kinds of hummingbirds in the world. Their brightly colored feathers make them look **handsome**. Do you know how these birds got their name? When they beat their wings very quickly, the wings make a humming sound.

Reread the sentences where you see these words. What do you think each word means?

dainty: _____

hover: _____

handsome: _____

Name: _____ Date: _____

Read what each word means.
Then fill in each blank with the correct word.

> **dainty:** small and delicate
>
> **hover:** to stay in one place in the air
>
> **handsome:** good-looking

1. A helicopter can _____ in the air.

2. Julia had a _____ dollhouse filled with
tiny furniture.

3. With shiny black fur and a strong body, Rex is a

_____ dog.

 Draw something that is as dainty as a hummingbird.

Words in Context: Animals © Cynthia Williamson, Scholastic Inc.

Name: _____   Date: _____

Draw a line to match each word with its meaning.

handsome   • small and delicate

hover   • good-looking

dainty   • to stay in one place
                              in the air

Write a sentence using one of the vocabulary words.
(Your sentence should begin with a capital letter
and end with a period.)

_____

_____

BONUS Is it true that hummingbirds are the only birds that can fly backwards? (Check one.)

☐ Yes   ☐ No

Name: _____ Date: _____

Seagulls

It is **common** to see seagulls at the beach. These white birds have gray wings and yellow beaks. Seagulls can be very loud. They often **shriek** and fight with other birds. Their favorite food is small fish that they **pluck** from the sea. They also eat worms and insects. Sometimes seagulls will

steal leftover food from a picnic. Seagulls are one of very few animals that can drink salt water. Some can dive underwater for a short time, too.

Reread the sentences where you see these words. What do you think each word means?

common: _____

shriek: _____

pluck: _____

Words in Context: Animals © Cynthia Williamson, Scholastic Inc.

Name: _____   Date: _____

Read what each word means.
Then fill in each blank with the correct word.

common: happening often; not rare

shriek: to cry out in a high voice

pluck: to snatch or pull out

1. Bears are _____ in many parts of the world.

2. Let's _____ a ripe cherry from the tree.

3. Theo let out a loud _____ when I surprised him.

BONUS Draw a picture of something that would make you shriek!

Name: _____   Date: _____

Draw a line to match each word with its meaning.

shriek   • happening often; not rare

pluck   • to cry out in a high voice

common   • to snatch or pull out

Write a sentence using one of the vocabulary words.
(Your sentence should begin with a capital letter
and end with a period.)

_____

_____

BONUS **Is it true that most birds can drink salt water?** (Check one.)

☐ Yes   ☐ No

Name: _____   Date: _____

Turkeys

Do you live in the United States? Then you'll probably be eating a big turkey dinner in November. This tasty bird is often served on Thanksgiving Day. **Tame** turkeys are raised on farms, just like chickens and ducks. Wild turkeys live in forests.

Turkeys make many kinds of noises. The most **familiar** is the *gobble-gobble* of the male turkey. It can be heard by other turkeys up to a mile away. These gentle birds are **curious** and like to explore the world around them.

Reread the sentences where you see these words. What do you think each word means?

tame: _____

familiar: _____

curious: _____

Name: _____   Date: _____

Read what each word means.
Then fill in each blank with the correct word.

> **tame:** gentle; not shy
>
> **familiar:** well-known; often seen or heard
>
> **curious:** eager to learn

1. I am _____ about outer space.

2. A wolf is a wild animal, but most dogs are _____.

3. My mother's face is very _____ to me.

BONUS **List three things you are curious about.**

- _____

- _____

- _____

Words in Context: Animals © Cynthia Williamson, Scholastic Inc.

Name: _____   Date: _____

Draw a line to match each word with its meaning.

familiar   • eager to learn

curious   • well-known; often seen or heard

tame   • gentle; not shy

Write a sentence using one of the vocabulary words.
(Your sentence should begin with a capital letter
and end with a period.)

_____

_____

BONUS Is it true that turkeys can be tame or wild? (Check one.)

☐ Yes   ☐ No

Cumulative Review

Review the meaning of each vocabulary word below.

common: happening often; not rare

curious: eager to learn

dainty: small and delicate

familiar: well-known; often seen or heard

handsome: good-looking

hover: to stay in one place in the air

pluck: to snatch or pull out

shriek: to cry out in a high voice

tame: gentle; not shy

Words in Context: Animals © Cynthia Williamson, Scholastic Inc.

Name: _____   Date: _____

1. Write the meaning of each word. (25 points each)

handsome: _____

tame: _____

2. Pick one of the words below.
Write a sentence using that word. (50 points)

| common | hover | familiar | pluck |

_____

_____

BONUS **Is it true that turkeys make many different noises?** (+5 points)

☐ Yes   ☐ No

Getting to Know Our Feathered Friends

Try any of these activities to deepen children's learning of birds.

What makes a bird a bird? Gather photos of different kinds of animals—mammals, reptiles, insects, and birds. Show the class each photo and ask: *Is this a bird?* Make a T-chart on the board with the headings "Bird" and "Not a Bird" and give each child an animal photo to post under the correct heading. When all the photos have been sorted, have children look at the birds carefully. Ask them: *How did you know those animals were birds?* Guide children to describe birds' characteristics or attributes, such as feathers, wings, two legs, and beak. List these attributes on the chart.

How fast can you flap your arms? Tell children that a hummingbird can flap its wings about 50 times per second—that's about 3,000 times per minute. The fastest rate recorded was 80 times per second! Partner up children and challenge them to flap their wings (arms) as many times as they can in one minute. When you say, "Go" and start the timer, one child in each pair flaps his or her arms, while the partner counts how many until you call time. (Have children count only on the downbeat.) Then have partners switch roles. Afterwards, compare results. Then ask children how their arms feel. (Most will feel tired.) Explain that a bird's wings are adapted to that kind of movement—just like our legs are adapted to walking—so birds can flap their wings far longer than we can flap our arms.

Why are birds' beaks different? Show children pictures of different bird beaks, such as those of blue jays, cardinals, ducks, hummingbirds, woodpeckers, eagles, hawks, parrots, pelicans, flamingos, and more. Ask: *What do you notice about the beaks?* (They're all different shapes and sizes.) Explain that birds' beaks are shaped differently, depending on what they eat. For example, blue jays and cardinals have beaks that can crack nuts. Hummingbirds' long, pointy beaks can get nectar from long-necked flowers. Eagles and hawks have sharp, curved beaks that can tear into meat. Divide the class into small groups and provide each group with pliers, tweezers, shelled nuts,* and a small paper cup with bird seeds. Have children use the pliers and tweezers like beaks to get food. Which tool is better for grabbing bird seeds? Which tool is better for cracking open nuts?

*Always check for allergies.

Polar Bears

The polar bear is probably
the most familiar animal
we know that lives in
the icy Arctic. How does
it **survive** the freezing
weather? The polar bear
has a **dense** coat of fur.
Under its white fur is black
skin. The dark skin soaks
up heat from the sun. The
polar bear also has a thick layer of fat that keeps it warm.

The polar bear is the largest meat-eating mammal on Earth.
It can grow to be 10 feet tall. It can weigh more than 1,000
pounds. The polar bear is an excellent swimmer. It can paddle
with its **broad** paws for many, many miles! It can also run very
fast. Its long claws keep it from slipping on the ice.

**Reread the sentences where you see these words.
What do you think each word means?**

survive: _____

dense: _____

broad: _____

Name: _____   Date: _____

Read what each word means.
Then fill in each blank with the correct word.

> **survive:** to stay alive
>
> **dense:** thick and packed together
>
> **broad:** wide and large

1. Few animals can _____ in the dry desert.

2. Six kids can sit side-by-side on the _____ couch.

3. We could barely see through the _____ fog.

BONUS **Draw a picture of a place where a polar bear could NOT survive.**

Words in Context: Animals © Cynthia Williamson, Scholastic Inc.

Draw a line to match each word with its meaning.

survive   • wide and large

dense   • to stay alive

broad   • thick and packed together

Write a sentence using one of the vocabulary words.
(Your sentence should begin with a capital letter
and end with a period.)

_____

_____

BONUS Is it true that polar bears live in jungles? (Check one.)

☐ Yes   ☐ No

Narwhals

Do you know what a unicorn is? It's a magical **creature** that looks like a horse. It has a long, sharp horn on top of its head. The unicorn is not real, but the narwhal is.

The narwhal is a type of whale that lives in icy Arctic waters. It has a long **tusk** that grows from the top of its head. That's why some people call it "unicorn of the sea." We don't know how the narwhal uses its tusk. But some think it helps the whale **sense** changes in the water around it. Most narwhals are black or gray in color. But as they get older, their smooth skin turns white. Like all whales, narwhals breathe air and grow very large.

Reread the sentences where you see these words. What do you think each word means?

creature: _____

tusk: _____

sense: _____

Read what each word means.
Then fill in each blank with the correct word.

> **creature:** a living thing, human or animal
>
> **tusk:** a long, pointed tooth
>
> **sense:** to feel or be aware of something

1. Your dentist would be surprised if you grew

a _____.

2. The furry _____ lived in the forest.

3. Some animals can _____ when an
enemy is near.

 BONUS **Make a list of creatures that live in a forest near you or that you've read about.**

- _____

- _____

- _____

Draw a line to match each word with its meaning.

tusk   • a living thing, human or animal

creature   • to feel or be aware of something

sense   • a long, pointed tooth

Write a sentence using one of the vocabulary words.
(Your sentence should begin with a capital letter
and end with a period.)

_____

_____

BONUS **Is it true that we know how narwhals use their tusks?**
(Check one.)

☐ Yes   ☐ No

Cumulative Review

Review the meaning of each vocabulary word below.

broad: wide and large

creature: a living thing, human or animal

dense: thick and packed together

sense: to feel or be aware of something

survive: to stay alive

tusk: a long, pointed tooth

Name: _____ Date: _____

1. Write the meaning of each word. (25 points each)

broad: _____

creature: _____

2. Pick one of the words below.
Write a sentence using that word. (50 points)

| sense | survive | dense | tusk |

_____

_____

BONUS Is it true that narwhals are called "unicorns of the sea?"
(+5 points)

☐ Yes   ☐ No

Camouflage Collage

Children camouflage animals to hide them from enemies.

YOU'LL NEED

- crayons and markers
- drawing paper
- scissors
- old magazines (especially *National Geographic*)
- glue
- cotton balls

TO DO

1 Ask children: *Why do you think polar bears and many other Arctic animals, like snowy owls, Arctic foxes, and snowshoe hares, are white?* (Some children will likely realize that being white helps an animal blend into its snowy environment.) Explain that this is called *camouflage*, and it helps many animals hide from predators and stay safe.

2 Tell children that they will be making a camouflage collage featuring an Arctic animal in its natural habitat. Explain that a collage is a picture made from different kinds of materials.

3 Have children draw their animal or cut out a picture of an Arctic animal from a magazine.

4 Finally, have them "camouflage" their animal by gluing cotton balls onto their picture.

EXTRA ACTIVITY

Demonstrate how blubber helps Arctic animals, like polar bears, stay warm. Put some shortening in a sandwich-size plastic zip-lock bag. Then turn another zip-lock bag inside out and put it inside the first bag so that the shortening is sandwiched between the bags. Squeeze out the air, then zip the bags together. Make another double layer of plastic bags (without shortening) for control. Put ice-cold water in a deep bowl or pan. Have a child put one hand in the "blubber" bag and the other hand in the plain plastic bag. Plunge both hands in the water. Ask: *Which hand feels colder?*

Marmosets

How can you tell a monkey from an ape? Look for a tail! Monkeys have tails, but apes do not. The marmoset is the smallest monkey in the world, but it has a very long tail. These animals **scamper** high in the jungle treetops.

There are about 20 different kinds of marmosets. Most of them could fit in an adult's hand. The most common type of marmoset is the cotton-eared marmoset. It has a **tuft** of white hair on each ear. Some people think these **appealing** little creatures would make good pets. But they are wrong. Marmosets are wild animals, not pets.

**Reread the sentences where you see these words.
What do you think each word means?**

scamper: _____

tuft: _____

appealing: _____

Name: _____ **Date:** _____

Read what each word means.
Then fill in each blank with the correct word.

> **scamper:** to run with light, quick steps
>
> **tuft:** a bunch of something, like hair, growing close together
>
> **appealing:** cute; easy to like

1. I pulled a _____ of weeds from the garden.

2. The kitten likes to _____ up and down the stairs.

3. Most of us think that puppies are very _____.

 Draw a picture of something that you find appealing.

Name: _____   Date: _____

Draw a line to match each word with its meaning.

scamper   • cute; easy to like

appealing   • a bunch of something, like hair,
                                       growing close together

tuft   • to run with light, quick steps

Write a sentence using one of the vocabulary words.
(Your sentence should begin with a capital letter
and end with a period.)

_____

_____

BONUS **Is it true that marmosets make great pets?** (Check one.)

☐ Yes   ☐ No

Words in Context: Animals © Cynthia Williamson, Scholastic Inc.

Mountain Gorillas

Mountain gorillas are **rare**. They can be found only in the **misty** mountains of Africa. These large apes are playful and smart. They live in groups called *troops*. These strong creatures **protect** one another.

Fully grown males have fur the color of silver on their backs. Their arms are longer than their legs. That's why mountain gorillas walk on their knuckles. They need to eat up to 50 pounds of food every day. They spend most of their time searching for fruit and insects to eat.

Reread the sentences where you see these words.
What do you think each word means?

rare: _____

misty: _____

protect: _____

Name: _____   Date: _____

Read what each word means.
Then fill in each blank with the correct word.

> **rare:** not often seen or found
>
> **misty:** foggy
>
> **protect:** to keep safe from harm

1. The mother dog wanted to _____ her puppies.

2. It was _____ on the beach this morning.

3. The tiger is a _____ animal from Asia.

BONUS **Draw a picture of something that is rare.**

Words in Context: Animals © Cynthia Williamson, Scholastic Inc.

Name: _____   Date: _____

Draw a line to match each word with its meaning.

rare   • to keep safe from harm

protect   • foggy

misty   • not often seen or found

Write a sentence using one of the vocabulary words.
(Your sentence should begin with a capital letter
and end with a period.)

_____

_____

BONUS **Is it true that a group of gorillas is called a *troop*?**
(Check one.)

☐ Yes   ☐ No

Gibbons

Gibbons have the **ability** to swing from tree to tree. They use their **slender**, strong arms. These small apes have powerful voices. Their howls and shrieks **echo** in the quiet jungles of Asia. Gibbons have thick, soft fur that can be gold or black. These handsome animals spend most of their time in the treetops. They even sleep up there. But when gibbons come down to earth,

they walk on two legs. Just like gorillas, these apes live in close family groups. They play together and protect one another.

Reread the sentences where you see these words. What do you think each word means?

ability: _____

slender: _____

echo: _____

Read what each word means.
Then fill in each blank with the correct word.

> **ability:** skill; power to do something
>
> **slender:** thin; slim
>
> **echo:** a sound that repeats itself

1. I heard the _____ of our voices in the dark cave.

2. The strong wind almost knocked down the

_____ trees.

3. I have the _____ to read and spell.

BONUS **Complete this sentence:**

I am proud of my ability to _____

_____ .

Name: _____   Date: _____

Draw a line to match each word with its meaning.

ability   • thin; slim

echo   • skill; power to do something

slender   • a sound that repeats itself

Write a sentence using one of the vocabulary words.
(Your sentence should begin with a capital letter
and end with a period.)

_____

_____

BONUS Is it true that gibbons live in the mountains of South America?
(Check one.)

☐ Yes   ☐ No

Name: _____ Date: _____

Cumulative Review

Review the meaning of each vocabulary word below.

ability: skill; power to do something

appealing: cute; easy to like

echo: a sound that repeats itself

misty: foggy

protect: to keep safe from harm

rare: not often seen or found

scamper: to run with light, quick steps

slender: thin; slim

tuft: a bunch of something, like hair, growing close together

Name: _____ Date: _____

1. Write the meaning of each word. (25 points each)

scamper: _____

misty: _____

2. Pick one of the words below.
   Write a sentence using that word. (50 points)

| echo | tuft | protect | slender |

_____

_____

BONUS Is it true that tiny marmosets live in deserts? (+5 points)

☐ Yes   ☐ No

Hand-in-Hand With a Gorilla

Children compare the size of their hands with that of a gorilla's.

YOU'LL NEED
- *Actual Size*, by Steve Jenkins
- pink paint
- construction paper
- scissors
- glue sticks

TO DO

1 Make a copy of the gorilla handprint on page 19 of the picture book *Actual Size*, by Steve Jenkins, for each child. Read the book aloud to the class.

2 Help each child paint his or her left hand with pink paint and then make a handprint inside the larger gorilla handprint.

3 Cut out the handprints and mount them on heavy construction paper.

4 Have children compare and contrast their handprint with that of the gorilla's.

TAKE IT FURTHER

As a class, discuss how apes and humans are alike and how they are different.

Snow Leopards

Snow leopards live high in the snowy mountains of Asia. These wild cats have thick, silky white or gray fur with black spots. They have very long, fluffy tails. When a snow leopard sleeps, it wraps its tail around its body like a blanket. This helps keep it warm.

Snow leopards are sometimes called "ghost cats." That's because their pale fur makes them hard to see in a rocky **landscape**. This makes them **effective** hunters. The mothers care for their young for about two years. Then the young cats learn to **fend** for themselves. They live most of their lives alone.

Reread the sentences where you see these words. What do you think each word means?

landscape: _____

effective: _____

fend: _____

Read what each word means.
Then fill in each blank with the correct word.

> **landscape:** a large area of land
>
> **effective:** something that works well
>
> **fend:** to care for

1. Baby animals are unable to _____ for themselves.

2. Asking questions is an _____ way to learn.

3. From the window of the train, I saw the green

_____ of the countryside.

 Draw a picture of a landscape, such as your yard or a city park.

Draw a line to match each word with its meaning.

landscape   • to care for

effective   • a large area of land

fend   • something that works well

Write a sentence using one of the vocabulary words.
(Your sentence should begin with a capital letter
and end with a period.)

_____

_____

BONUS **Is it true that snow leopards are sometimes called "ghost cats?"** (Check one.)

☐ Yes   ☐ No

Cheetahs

The cheetah is the fastest land animal in the world. It races across the grassy African landscape to catch **prey**. Its long, strong tail helps it make quick turns as it runs. Its spotted fur helps it blend in with the tall grass. The

cheetah has black stripes under each eye. They keep the **glare** of the sun out of its eyes. This helps it focus on its prey. All of these features help make the cheetah a very effective hunter. It gets a lot of **respect** from other animals.

Reread the sentences where you see these words.
What do you think each word means?

prey: _____

glare: _____

respect: _____

Name: _____   Date: _____

Read what each word means.
Then fill in each blank with the correct word.

> **prey:** an animal hunted by another animal for food
>
> **glare:** very bright light
>
> **respect:** a feeling of admiration and awe for someone

1. Elaina felt _____ for Sam when she saw him help a homeless person.

2. The flashlight's _____ helped us see in the dark.

3. The silent owl flew down to catch its _____.

 What's another thing that gives off a glare?

_____

Words in Context: Animals © Cynthia Williamson, Scholastic Inc.

Name: _____   Date: _____

Draw a line to match each word with its meaning.

prey   • very bright light

respect   • an animal hunted by another
                                          animal for food

glare   • a feeling of admiration
                                          and awe for someone

Write a sentence using one of the vocabulary words.
(Your sentence should begin with a capital letter
and end with a period.)

_____

_____

BONUS **Complete this sentence:**

Cheetahs live on the grasslands of _____.

Name: _____   **Date:** _____

Rusty-Spotted Cats

The rusty-spotted cat is the tiniest of the wild cats. It lives in India and Sri Lanka. This big-eyed beauty looks much like our pet cats, but smaller. It weighs only two to three pounds. The rusty-spotted cat has short legs and gray fur with dark

spots. Its long tail is a bit darker. It is often **mistaken** for a baby leopard. This wild cat may be little and cute, but it can be very **brave** when hunting for food. Some say there are fewer than 10,000 of these creatures on Earth. But others think they may be far more **numerous**.

Reread the sentences where you see these words. What do you think each word means?

mistaken _____

brave: _____

numerous: _____

Name: _____   Date: _____

Read what each word means.
Then fill in each blank with the correct word.

> **mistaken:** was wrong about something
>
> **brave:** willing to face danger or fear
>
> **numerous:** made up of a large number

1. There are _____ cars on the busy highway.

2. I was _____ about how to spell a word.

3. The _____ firefighters rushed into the burning building.

 Complete this sentence:

I showed how brave I can be when I _____

_____.

Draw a line to match each word with its meaning.

brave   • made up of a large number

mistaken   • was wrong about something

numerous   • willing to face danger or fear

Write a sentence using one of the vocabulary words.
(Your sentence should begin with a capital letter
and end with a period.)

_____

_____

BONUS **Is it true that the rusty-spotted cat is often mistaken for a baby leopard?** (Check one.)

☐ Yes   ☐ No

Words in Context: Animals © Cynthia Williamson, Scholastic Inc.

Name: _____   Date: _____

Cumulative Review

Review the meaning of each vocabulary word below.

brave: willing to face danger or fear

effective: something that works well

fend: to care for

glare: very bright light

landscape: a large area of land

mistaken: was wrong about something

numerous: made up of a large number

prey: an animal hunted by another animal for food

respect: a feeling of admiration and awe for someone

Name: _____ Date: _____

1. Write the meaning of each word. (25 points each)

effective: _____

respect: _____

2. Pick one of the words below.
Write a sentence using that word. (50 points)

numerous	fend	prey	mistaken

_____

_____

BONUS **Is it true that cheetahs can run faster than any other animal on Earth?** (+5 points)

☐ Yes   ☐ No

Kitty Feathers

Show children how to make this easy, fun toy for cats.

YOU'LL NEED
- brown or gold felt
- scissors
- hole punch
- small jingle bells
- string or yarn

TO DO

1 Cut a feather shape from the felt, one for each child.
Punch a small hole in the stem of the feather.

2 Have children cut fringes along the edges of the felt feather.
Make sure they don't cut too far toward the center.

3 Show children how to attach a bell to a length of string or yarn.
Thread the bell and string through the hole in the stem of the
feather. The string or yarn should be long enough to dangle in
front of a cat, which will love batting at the toy with its paws.

4 Allow children to bring the kitty toy home for their own pet
or to give to a friend's pet.

Sheep

Farm animals are not the same as wild animals or pets. They are raised on farms to **provide** food and clothing for people.

Sheep are a good example. These common farm animals grow thick coats of wool. The wool can be made into cloth. Adult male sheep are called *rams*. They have large horns that **curve** around their faces. Adult females are known as *ewes*. The milk of ewes can be made into tasty cheese and creamy yogurt. Baby sheep are called *lambs*. Numerous types of sheep live on farms around the world. There are even **miniature** sheep, which are less than two feet tall. They are called "babydoll" sheep.

Reread the sentences where you see these words. What do you think each word means?

provide: _____

curve: _____

miniature: _____

Name: _____   Date: _____

Read what each word means.
Then fill in each blank with the correct word.

> **provide:** to give something that someone needs
>
> **curve:** to bend
>
> **miniature:** smaller than usual in size

1. My dollhouse is a _____ version of our home.

2. Some farm animals _____ food for us.

3. Instead of going straight, the roads in our neighborhood

_____.

BONUS **Draw a picture of something miniature.**

Draw a line to match each word with its meaning.

curve   • smaller than usual in size

provide   • to give something that
                                           someone needs

miniature   • to bend

Write a sentence using one of the vocabulary words.

_____

_____

 Complete the sentence below.

Baby sheep are called _____.

Words in Context: Animals © Cynthia Williamson, Scholastic Inc.

Ostriches

You've probably seen cows, pigs, and chickens on a farm. But have you seen a **pasture** full of ostriches? Today, there are many ostrich farms around the world. Ostriches are raised for their eggs, meat, and feathers. One pale-yellow ostrich egg is

equal to two dozen chicken eggs. Long ago, ostrich feathers were used to **decorate** hats. Their feathers are still used in fashion today.

Ostriches can grow to be 9 feet tall. They have long necks and large eyes with curly eyelashes. These **husky** birds are too heavy to fly. But they are very fast runners.

Reread the sentences where you see these words. What do you think each word means?

pasture: _____

decorate: _____

husky: _____

Name: _____   Date: _____

Read what each word means.
Then fill in each blank with the correct word.

> **pasture:** land where farm animals graze
>
> **decorate:** to make something look prettier
>
> **husky:** large and strong

1. Cows nibbled on grass in the green _____.

2. The hippo is a _____ animal.

3. We can _____ our classroom with colorful
pictures and posters.

BONUS **Make a list of things you can decorate.**

- _____
- _____
- _____

Words in Context: Animals © Cynthia Williamson, Scholastic Inc.

Draw a line to match each word with its meaning.

husky   • to make something look prettier

decorate   • land where farm animals graze

pasture   • large and strong

Write a sentence using one of the vocabulary words.

_____

_____

BONUS Is it true that ostriches can grow to be more than 100 feet tall? (Check one.)

☐ Yes   ☐ No

Camels

There are camel farms around the world. Most of them are in Africa and India. Caring for a herd of camels is an **expensive** job. They need large shelters with high ceilings. The shelters can cost a lot

of money to build. Camels also need broad pastures so they can get proper **exercise**.

Farmers say camels are not easy to raise. Some of these tall creatures with the well-known humps are calm and gentle. But others kick and spit when farmers try to milk them. Some people say camel milk is healthier than milk from cows or goats. Camels' **lean** meat tastes like beef.

Reread the sentences where you see these words.
What do you think each word means?

expensive: _____

exercise: _____

lean: _____

Name: _____   Date: _____

Read what each word means.
Then fill in each blank with the correct word.

expensive: costing a lot of money

exercise: physical activity that makes the body fit and healthy

lean: having little or no fat

1. We get a lot of _____ during gym class.

2. Our vacation was _____ but we had a lot of fun.

3. We had a _____ meal of soup and salad.

BONUS **Draw a picture of your favorite way to exercise.**

Name: _____   Date: _____

Draw a line to match each word with its meaning.

lean   • costing a lot of money

expensive   • physical activity that makes
                                    the body fit and healthy

exercise   • having little or no fat

Write a sentence using one of the vocabulary words.

_____

_____

BONUS **Is it true that raising camels is easy?** (Check one.)

☐ Yes   ☐ No

Words in Context: Animals © Cynthia Williamson, Scholastic Inc.

Name: _____   Date: _____

Cumulative Review

Review the meaning of each vocabulary word below.

curve: to bend

decorate: to make something look prettier

exercise: physical activity that makes the body fit and healthy

expensive: costing a lot of money

husky: large and strong

lean: having little or no fat

miniature: smaller than usual in size

pasture: land where farm animals graze

provide: to give something that someone needs

1. Write the meaning of each word. (25 points each)

pasture: _____

expensive: _____

2. Pick one of the words below.
   Write a sentence using that word. (50 points)

husky	curve	provide	lean

_____

_____

BONUS Is it true that female sheep are called *ewes?* (+5 points)

☐ Yes   ☐ No

Cotton Sheep

Kids will enjoy making sheep out of cotton balls.

YOU'LL NEED

- pictures of sheep
- classroom projection system
- crayons and markers
- construction paper
- glue sticks
- cotton balls (or plain popcorn)

TO DO

1 If you can, project a few pictures of sheep for children's reference.

2 Using crayons and markers, have children draw a sheep on construction paper.

3 When children are finished with their drawings, have them create a coat of woolly fleece by gluing cotton balls (or plain popcorn) on their sheep's body.

TAKE IT FURTHER

Have children give examples of clothing made from wool. Then, go online to research how people make clothes from wool. With the class, watch videos of sheep shearing, wool carding, and other steps in the process.

Dogs

Do you have a dog? Dogs are one of the most **popular** pets in the world. Some dogs are tiny. Others are **enormous**. Many people who live in cities choose small dogs, like pugs. Those who live on a farm or in the country may have big dogs, such as German shepherds.

Puppies are very cute, but they **require** a lot of care. Like older dogs, they need a warm place to sleep, fresh food, exercise, and lots of love. Puppies also need to be trained. This helps them know how to behave around people and other animals. If you train your dog well, you'll have a good friend for many years.

Reread the sentences where you see these words.
What do you think each word means?

popular: _____

enormous: _____

require: _____

Read what each word means.
Then fill in each blank with the correct word.

> **popular:** liked by many people
>
> **enormous:** very large
>
> **require:** to need something

1. Pizza is the most _____ food served
in our lunchroom.

2. Kids _____ at least nine hours of sleep
every night.

3. Polar bears have _____ paws.

BONUS **Make a list of games that are popular at birthday parties.**

- _____

- _____

- _____

- _____

- _____

Name: _____   Date: _____

Draw a line to match each word with its meaning.

enormous   • to need something

require   • very large

popular   • liked by many people

Write a sentence using one of the vocabulary words.

_____

_____

 BONUS **A German shepherd is an example of a big dog. What is an example of a small dog?**

_____

Words in Context: Animals © Cynthia Williamson, Scholastic Inc.

Tortoises

Tortoises may not be as popular as dogs and cats. But many people keep these slow-moving animals as pets. Tortoises have thick, colorful shells and wide, flat feet. They can be **timid**. They **retreat** into their shells when scared. If you **decide** to keep a

tortoise as a pet, every day you will need to give it fresh fruit and plenty of water. Make sure your tortoise never gets too cold. Give it a bath in warm water once a week. Tortoises can live very long lives. Some live to be 100 years old!

Reread the sentences where you see these words. What do you think each word means?

timid: _____

retreat: _____

decide: _____

Read what each word means.
Then fill in each blank with the correct word.

> **timid:** shy or fearful
>
> **retreat:** to move back and hide
>
> **decide:** to make up your mind about something

1. Many of us feel _____ on the first day of school.

2. I can't _____ if I want to ride my bike
or shoot hoops.

3. I _____ to my tree house when my brother
teases me.

BONUS **What could you do to help a classmate who is feeling timid?**

_____

_____

Draw a line to match each word with its meaning.

decide   • shy or fearful

retreat   • to make up your mind
                                      about something

timid   • to move back and hide

Write a sentence using one of the vocabulary words.

_____

_____

BONUS

Is it true that some tortoises can live to be 100 years old?
(Check one.)

☐ Yes   ☐ No

Alpacas

Peru is a country in South
America. There, some boys and
girls keep alpacas as pets. This
charming animal has a long
neck and soft fur. A full-grown
alpaca stands about 3 feet tall.
Some say it looks like a small
llama or camel. Alpacas are
gentle and playful, but not timid.
They rarely bite, but they will
kick and spit at you if you **annoy**
them. Caring for an alpaca is
easy. These **hearty** animals can
live in cold or warm weather. They eat all kinds of fruits,
vegetables, and grains. Wouldn't it be fun to have a pet alpaca?

**Reread the sentences where you see these words.
What do you think each word means?**

charming: _____

annoy: _____

hearty: _____

Name: _____   Date: _____

Read what each word means.
Then fill in each blank with the correct word.

> **charming:** very pleasing
>
> **annoy:** to bother or make someone angry
>
> **hearty:** strong and healthy

1. I _____ my big sister when I follow
her everywhere.

2. Since Dante is _____, he rarely gets sick.

3. Lisa is very _____, so it's easy for her
to make friends.

BONUS **What does your face look like when somebody annoys
you? Draw a picture of it below.**

Name: _____   Date: _____

Draw a line to match each word with its meaning.

charming   • strong and healthy

hearty   • to bother or make
                              someone angry

annoy   • very pleasing

Write a sentence using one of the vocabulary words.

_____

_____

BONUS

Peru is a country in: (Check one.)

☐ Asia   ☐ Africa   ☐ South America

Words in Context: Animals © Cynthia Williamson, Scholastic Inc.

Cumulative Review

Review the meaning of each vocabulary word below.

annoy: to bother or make someone angry

charming: very pleasing

decide: to make up your mind about something

enormous: very large

hearty: strong and healthy

popular: liked by many people

require: to need something

retreat: to move back and hide

timid: shy or fearful

1. Write the meaning of each word. (25 points each)

decide: _____

charming: _____

2. Pick one of the words below.
   Write a sentence using that word. (50 points)

retreat	enormous	require	hearty

_____

_____

BONUS **Is it true that alpacas are taller than camels?** (+5 points)

☐ Yes   ☐ No

Make Dog Biscuits

If you have a school kitchen your class can use, try this recipe for dog biscuits.

YOU'LL NEED

- 1 cube of beef or chicken bouillon
- ½ cup hot water
- 2 ½ cups of whole wheat flour
- 1 egg
- 1 tsp baking powder

TO DO

1 Preheat oven to 350 degrees.

2 Dissolve the bouillon in a bowl of hot water.

3 Add the other ingredients to the bouillon mixture. Knead to make dough.

4 Roll the dough to ½-inch thick.

5 Cut the flattened dough into slices (or use a bone-shaped cookie cutter).

6 Place the sliced dough on a lightly greased cookie sheet.

7 Bake for 30 minutes.

Allow children to bring the dog biscuits home to their own pets or to give to a friend's pet.

Maned Wolves

The maned wolf is the tallest wild dog
in South America. Maned wolves are
sometimes called "foxes on **stilts**." That's
because they have very long legs. That
helps them **pounce** when hunting for
food in the grasslands. These **peculiar**
animals have shaggy reddish-brown fur.
They have long, dark hair that runs from
their neck to their upper back. This mane
stands up straight when the wolf senses
danger nearby. Maned wolves do not
howl or live in packs. Instead, they live in
pairs. They raise their pups in cozy shelters.
Their loud voice sounds like both a bark and a roar.

**Reread the sentences where you see these words.
What do you think each word means?**

stilts: _____

pounce: _____

peculiar: _____

Name: _____   Date: _____

Read what each word means.
Then fill in each blank with the correct word.

stilts: a pair of poles used for walking on high above the ground

pounce: to jump on something suddenly

peculiar: odd; strange

1. When the clown walked on _____, he was almost 10 feet tall!

2. Our kitten will sometimes _____ on a ball of yarn.

3. I saw a _____ butterfly that looked like it had an owl's eyes.

BONUS **Complete this sentence:**

I find it peculiar that _____

_____.

Draw a line to match each word with its meaning.

peculiar   • a pair of poles used for walking
                              on high above the ground

pounce   • odd; strange

stilts   • to jump on something suddenly

Write a sentence using one of the vocabulary words.

_____

_____

BONUS **Is it true that maned wolves howl?** (Check one.)

☐ Yes   ☐ No

Words in Context: Animals © Cynthia Williamson, Scholastic Inc.

Gray Wolves

Gray wolves **roam** in forests around the world. They are the largest **members** of the dog family. They have bushy tails and sharp fangs. Gray wolves live in groups called *packs*. These **clever** hunters work together to pounce on large prey. Each pack has a male and

a female leader. They are the first to eat after a hunt. They are also the only ones to produce pups. A pack can have up to 20 wolves.

**Reread the sentences where you see these words.
What do you think each word means?**

roam: _____

members: _____

clever: _____

Read what each word means.
Then fill in each blank with the correct word.

> **roam:** to go from place to place
>
> **members:** people, animals, or things that belong to a group
>
> **clever:** smart and skillful

1. My whole family are _____ of the library.

2. It's fun to _____ around the quiet forest.

3. Jamie is quick and _____ in math, but spelling is hard for him.

BONUS **Draw a picture of a place where you'd like to roam.**

Name: _____   Date: _____

Draw a line to match each word with its meaning.

clever   • to go from place to place

roam   • people, animals, or things that
                                  belong to a group

members   • smart and skillful

Write a sentence using one of the vocabulary words.

_____

_____

Write a sentence using a different vocabulary word.

_____

_____

 Complete the sentence:

A group of wolves that live and hunt together is called

a _____.

Red Foxes

Red foxes live in different kinds of places. They can be found in deserts and forests. They can survive on mountains and in the icy Arctic. They can even **adapt** to live in large cities. This **sly** hunter feeds on small animals, like

rabbits and rats. It also eats plants and berries. It may even eat pet foods and raid garbage bins for tasty leftovers. Farmers **complain** that red foxes break into chicken coops. The foxes steal and feed on the helpless birds.

Reread the sentences where you see these words.
What do you think each word means?

adapt: _____

sly: _____

complain: _____

Words in Context: Animals © Cynthia Williamson, Scholastic Inc.

Name: _____   Date: _____

Read what each word means.
Then fill in each blank with the correct word.

adapt: to change to fit into a different situation

sly: clever in a sneaky way

complain: to say you are angry or unhappy
about something

1. We _____ to cold weather by wearing heavy
coats, mittens, and hats.

2. Sam would always _____ about our weekly
math quizzes.

3. Akira had a _____ plan to get a second dessert.

BONUS **Make a list of things that you complain about.**

- _____

- _____

- _____

Draw a line to match each word with its meaning.

adapt   • clever in a sneaky way

complain   • to change to fit into
a different situation

sly   • to say you are angry or
unhappy about something

Write a sentence using one of the vocabulary words.

_____

_____

Write a sentence using a different vocabulary word.

_____

_____

BONUS **Can red foxes survive in the icy Arctic?** (Check one.)

☐ Yes   ☐ No

                Words in Context: Animals © Cynthia Williamson, Scholastic Inc.

Name: _____ Date: _____

Cumulative Review

Review the meaning of each vocabulary word below.

adapt: to change to fit into a different situation

clever: smart and skillful

complain: to say you are angry or unhappy about something

members: people, animals, or things that belong to a group

peculiar: odd; strange

pounce: to jump on something suddenly

roam: to go from place to place

sly: clever in a sneaky way

stilts: a pair of poles used for walking on high above the ground

1. Write the meaning of each word. (25 points each)

clever: _____

pounce: _____

2. Pick one of the words below.
   Write a sentence using that word. (50 points)

sly	livestock	adapt	stilts

_____

_____

BONUS **Is it true that wolves live in packs with male and female leaders?** (+5 points)

☐ Yes   ☐ No

Fox Socks

Children make fox hand puppets out of old socks.

YOU'LL NEED

- *Fox in Socks*, by Dr. Seuss
- clean, old socks*
- scissors
- reddish-brown felt
- fabric glue
- googly eyes
- black pompoms
- markers

* Ask children to bring in a clean sock from home. Have extras for those who don't bring them in.

TO DO

1 Read aloud the book *Fox in Socks*, by Dr. Seuss.

2 Tell children they are going to make their own fox puppets out of old socks. Make sure each child has a clean, old sock to work with.

3 Cut triangles from felt to make the foxes' ears.

4 Have children put the sock on their hand. Then have them glue the ears, googly eyes, and black pompoms (nose) onto their sock puppets. Use markers to draw in a mouth and further decorate the foxes' faces. (Having children put the sock on their hand helps with the proper placement of these features.)

TAKE IT FURTHER

Invite children to take turns reading aloud the rhymes from the book in the voice of their sock puppets.

Name: _____   Date: _____

Chameleons

Snakes, lizards, crocodiles, and turtles are all examples of *reptiles*. Reptiles are cold-blooded animals that can live on land or in water. They all have a **spine** along their back. Most reptiles lay eggs with soft shells.

The chameleon is one of the most interesting types of lizards. It has big, **bulging** eyes. The eyes can look in two different directions at the same time. Most amazingly, the chameleon can change colors. It may do this to hide from other animals that want to eat it. It may also change colors to send signals to other chameleons. The chameleon has a long, sticky tongue. It shoots out from its mouth very quickly to catch a passing insect. Chameleons prefer a warm **climate.** They can be found in deserts as well as jungles.

Reread the sentences where you see these words. What do you think each word means?

spine: _____

bulging: _____

climate: _____

Words in Context: Animals © Cynthia Williamson, Scholastic Inc.

Name: _____ Date: _____

Read what each word means.
Then fill in each blank with the correct word.

spine: backbone, which goes from an animal's skull to its lower back

bulging: sticking out

climate: the usual weather in a place

1. My grandparents live in a warm _____ and rarely see snow.

2. Mammals have a _____, but jellyfish do not.

3. Mikey's bag was _____ with all the books he took out from the library.

BONUS **Draw a picture of an animal that lives in a cold climate.**

Draw a line to match each word with its meaning.

climate   • sticking out

bulging   • backbone, which goes from an animal's skull to its lower back

spine   • the usual weather in a place

Write a sentence using one of the vocabulary words.

_____

_____

Write a sentence using a different vocabulary word.

_____

_____

BONUS **Chameleons can be found in _____. (Check one.)**

☐ **deserts**   ☐ **jungles**   ☐ **both**

                                   Words in Context: Animals © Cynthia Williamson, Scholastic Inc.

Name: _____ Date: _____

Snakes

Different kinds of snakes live around the world. In swampy places, water moccasins swim in the still, fresh water. These **bold** snakes have long fangs and a deadly bite. Avoid them!

Stay away from rattlesnakes, too. These legless reptiles often soak up the sun in the hot, dry desert. If you come too close, a rattlesnake shakes the rattle at the tip of its long body. It makes a **startling** sound. Get away quickly or **risk** being bitten.

Both water moccasins and rattlesnakes are dangerous. But most snakes are harmless. Garter snakes, for example, help keep pests out of gardens. Some people keep snakes as pets. Would you?

**Reread the sentences where you see these words.
What do you think each word means?**

bold: _____

startling: _____

risk: _____

Name: _____   Date: _____

Read what each word means.
Then fill in each blank with the correct word.

> **bold:** brave; fearless
>
> **startling:** causing surprise or shock
>
> **risk:** to take a chance

1. It was _____ to hear the fire alarm ringing
in the middle of the night.

2. The _____ puppy ran into the road and almost
got hit by a car.

3. Lifeguards _____ their lives to save people
from drowning.

 Draw a picture of your face when you see something startling.

Words in Context: Animals © Cynthia Williamson, Scholastic Inc.

Draw a line to match each word with its meaning.

startling   • causing surprise or shock

bold   • to take a chance

risk   • brave; fearless

Write a sentence for each vocabulary word.

• _____

  _____

• _____

  _____

• _____

  _____

BONUS Is it true that most snakes are harmless, but rattlesnakes
can be dangerous? (Check one.)

☐ Yes   ☐ No

Cumulative Review

Review the meaning of each vocabulary word below.

bold: brave; fearless

bulging: sticking out

climate: the usual weather in a place

risk: to take a chance

spine: backbone, which goes from an animal's skull to its lower back

startling: causing surprise or shock

Words in Context: Animals © Cynthia Williamson, Scholastic Inc.

1. Write the meaning of each word. (25 points each)

bold: _____

climate: _____

2. Pick one of the words below.
   Write a sentence using that word. (50 points)

risk	bulging	startling	spine

_____

_____

BONUS **Is it true that chameleons can look in two different directions at the same time?** (+5 points)

☐ Yes   ☐ No

Paper-Plate Snakes

Use bubble wrap to paint scales on paper-plate snakes.

YOU'LL NEED

- black permanent marker
- paper plates
- bubble wrap, cut into squares about 2-by-2 inches
- variety of colors of tempera paint
- tray

- construction paper
- scissors
- glue sticks
- googly eyes
- string

TO DO

1 Use a black permanent marker to draw a spiral shape on each paper plate, starting on the outside and ending in the center.

2 Give each child a paper plate and a square of bubble wrap.

3 Pour various colors of paint onto a flat surface, such as a tray or paper plate.

4 Have children dip the bubble wrap into the paint and dab it onto their paper plate. This creates the snake's scales.

5 From construction paper, cut out a head for the snake. Use red construction paper for the tongue.

6 Have children glue the head onto the middle of their paper plate. Have them glue on the googly eyes and the tongue as well.

7 Show children how to cut the paper plate along the spiral to create the snake's body. Tie a string around the head and hang from the ceiling.

Answer Key

WEEK 1-B (page 10)
1. clear **2.** avoid **3.** surface
Bonus: Sentences will vary.

WEEK 1-C (page 11)
clear —— to stay away from
surface —— easy to see through
avoid —— the top or outside part of something
Sentences will vary.
Bonus: Yes, a jellyfish's arms are called *tentacles.*

WEEK 2-B (page 13)
1. agree **2.** shallow **3.** odd
Bonus: Drawings will vary.

WEEK 2-C (page 14)
odd —— not deep
shallow —— to think the same way
agree —— strange; weird
Sentences will vary.
Bonus: Yes, seahorses can change their colors.

WEEK 3-B (page 16)
1. prowl **2.** shiver **3.** steady
Bonus: Drawings will vary.

WEEK 3-C (page 17)
shiver —— not changing
prowl —— to shake with cold or fear
steady —— to move around in a sneaky way
Sentences will vary.
Bonus: No, the basking shark does not eat other sharks.

WEEK 4, Assessment (page 19)
1. agree: to think the same way
  surface: the top or outside part of something
2. Sentences will vary.
Bonus: Yes, some seahorses swim together with their tails linked.

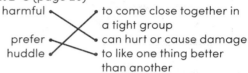

WEEK 1-B (page 22)
1. scarce **2.** cozy **3.** massive
Bonus: Drawings will vary.

WEEK 1-C (page 23)
scarce —— very large and heavy
massive —— warm and comfortable
cozy —— hard to find
Sentences will vary.
Bonus: Yes, bears can sleep for as long as seven months.

WEEK 2-B (page 25)
1. prefer **2.** huddle **3.** Harmful
Bonus: Answers will vary.

WEEK 2-C (page 26)
harmful —— to come close together in a tight group
prefer —— can hurt or cause damage
huddle —— to like one thing better than another
Sentences will vary.
Bonus: No, ladybugs are not harmful to our gardens.

WEEK 3-B (page 28)
1. nervous **2.** soar **3.** feast
Bonus: Answers will vary.

WEEK 3-C (page 29)
nervous —— to fly very high
soar —— feeling worried or afraid
feast —— to eat a lot of something
Sentences will vary.
Bonus: No, the smallest type of bat is the bumblebee bat.

WEEK 4, Assessment (page 31)
1. massive: very large and heavy
  soar: to fly very high
2. Sentences will vary.
Bonus: Yes, bats are mammals.

NOVEMBER

WEEK 1-B (page 34)
1. hover **2.** dainty **3.** handsome
Bonus: Drawings will vary.

WEEK 1-C (page 35)
handsome —— small and delicate
hover —— good-looking
dainty —— to stay in one place in the air
Sentences will vary.
Bonus: Yes, hummingbirds are the only birds that can fly backwards.

WEEK 2-B (page 37)
1. common **2.** pluck **3.** shriek
Bonus: Drawings will vary.

WEEK 2-C (page 38)
shriek —— happening often; not rare
pluck —— to cry out in a high voice
common —— to snatch or pull out
Sentences will vary.
Bonus: No, most birds cannot drink salt water.

WEEK 3-B (page 40)

1. curious **2.** tame **3.** familiar

Bonus: Answers will vary.

WEEK 3-C (page 41)

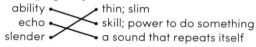

familiar — well-known; often seen or heard
curious — eager to learn
tame — gentle; not shy

Sentences will vary.

Bonus: Yes, turkeys can be tame or wild.

WEEK 4, Assessment (page 43)

1. handsome: good-looking
  tame: gentle; not shy

2. Sentences will vary.

Bonus: Yes, turkeys make many different noises.

DECEMBER

WEEK 1-B (page 46)

1. survive **2.** broad **3.** dense

Bonus: Drawings will vary.

WEEK 1-C (page 47)

survive — to stay alive
dense — wide and large
broad — thick and packed together

Sentences will vary.

Bonus: No, polar bears do not live in jungles.

WEEK 2-B (page 49)

1. tusk **2.** creature **3.** sense

Bonus: Answers will vary.

WEEK 2-C (page 50)

tusk — a living thing, human or animal
creature — to feel or be aware of something
sense — a long, pointed tooth

Sentences will vary.

Bonus: No, we don't know how narwhals use their tusks.

WEEK 3, Assessment (page 52)

1. broad: wide and large
  creature: a living thing, human or animal

2. Sentences will vary.

Bonus: Yes, narwhals are called "unicorns of the sea."

JANUARY

WEEK 1-B (page 55)

1. tuft **2.** scamper **3.** appealing

Bonus: Drawings will vary.

WEEK 1-C (page 56)

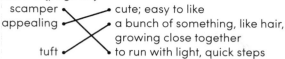

scamper — cute; easy to like
appealing — a bunch of something, like hair, growing close together
tuft — to run with light, quick steps

Sentences will vary.

Bonus: No, marmosets do not make great pets.

WEEK 2-B (page 58)

1. protect **2.** misty **3.** rare

Bonus: Drawings will vary.

WEEK 2-C (page 59)

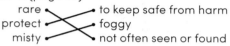

rare — to keep safe from harm
protect — foggy
misty — not often seen or found

Sentences will vary.

Bonus: Yes, a group of gorillas is called a *troop.*

WEEK 3-B (page 61)

1. echo **2.** slender **3.** ability

Bonus: Sentences will vary.

WEEK 3-C (page 62)

ability — thin; slim
echo — skill; power to do something
slender — a sound that repeats itself

Sentences will vary.

Bonus: No, gibbons do not live in the mountains of South America.

WEEK 4, Assessment (page 64)

1. scamper: to run with light, quick steps
  misty: foggy

2. Sentences will vary.

Bonus: No, marmosets do not live in deserts.

FEBRUARY

WEEK 1-B (page 67)

1. fend **2.** effective **3.** landscape

Bonus: Drawings will vary.

WEEK 1-C (page 68)

landscape — to care for
effective — a large area of land
fend — something that works well

Sentences will vary.

Bonus: Yes, snow leopards are called "ghost cats."

WEEK 2-B (page 70)

1. respect **2.** glare **3.** prey

Bonus: Answers will vary. Possible answers include headlights, flashlight, and light reflecting off water or snow.

WEEK 2-C (page 71)

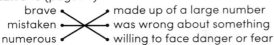

prey — an animal hunted by another animal for food
respect — a feeling of admiration and awe for someone
glare — very bright light

Sentences will vary.

Bonus: Cheetahs live on the grasslands of Africa.

WEEK 3-B (page 73)
1. numerous **2.** mistaken **3.** brave

Bonus: Sentences will vary.

WEEK 3-C (page 74)

brave — willing to face danger or fear
mistaken — was wrong about something
numerous — made up of a large number

Sentences will vary.

Bonus: Yes, the rusty-spotted cat is often mistaken for a baby leopard.

WEEK 4, Assessment (page 76)
1. effective: something that works well
   respect: a feeling of admiration and awe for someone

2. Sentences will vary.

Bonus: Yes, cheetahs can run faster than any other animal on Earth.

MARCH

WEEK 1-B (page 79)
1. miniature **2.** provide **3.** curve

Bonus: Drawings will vary.

WEEK 1-C (page 80)

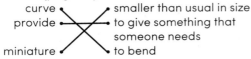

curve — to bend
provide — to give something that someone needs
miniature — smaller than usual in size

Sentences will vary.

Bonus: Baby sheep are called *lambs*.

WEEK 2-B (page 82)
1. pasture **2.** husky **3.** decorate

Bonus: Answers will vary.

WEEK 2-C (page 83)

husky — large and strong
decorate — to make something look prettier
pasture — land where farm animals graze

Sentences will vary.

Bonus: No, ostriches do not grow to be 100 feet tall.

WEEK 3-B (page 85)
1. exercise **2.** expensive **3.** lean

Bonus: Drawings will vary.

WEEK 3-C (page 86)

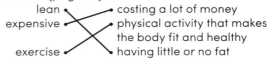

lean — having little or no fat
expensive — costing a lot of money
exercise — physical activity that makes the body fit and healthy

Sentences will vary.

Bonus: No, raising camels is not easy.

WEEK 4, Assessment (page 88)
1. pasture: land where farm animals graze
   expensive: costing a lot of money

2. Sentences will vary.

Bonus: Yes, female sheep are called *ewes*.

APRIL

WEEK 1-B (page 91)
1. popular **2.** require **3.** enormous

Bonus: Answers will vary.

WEEK 1-C (page 92)

enormous — very large
require — to need something
popular — liked by many people

Sentences will vary.

Bonus: Answers will vary. Possible answer: pug

WEEK 2-B (page 94)
1. timid **2.** decide **3.** retreat

Bonus: Answers will vary.

WEEK 2-C (page 95)

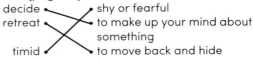

decide — to move back and hide
retreat — shy or fearful
timid — to make up your mind about something

Sentences will vary.

Bonus: Yes, some tortoises can live to be 100 years old.

WEEK 3-B (page 97)
1. annoy **2.** hearty **3.** charming

Bonus: Drawings will vary.

WEEK 3-C (page 98)

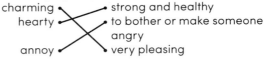

charming — very pleasing
hearty — strong and healthy
annoy — to bother or make someone angry

Sentences will vary.

Bonus: Peru is a country in South America.

WEEK 4, Assessment (page 100)
1. decide: to make up your mind about something
   charming: very pleasing

2. Sentences will vary.

Bonus: No, alpacas are not taller than camels.

WEEK 1-B (page 103)
1. stilts **2.** pounce **3.** peculiar
Bonus: Sentences will vary.

WEEK 1-C (page 104)

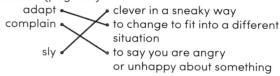

peculiar — a pair of poles used for walking on high above the ground
pounce — odd; strange
stilts — to jump on something suddenly

Sentences will vary.

Bonus: No, maned wolves do not howl.

WEEK 2-B (page 106)
1. members **2.** roam **3.** clever
Bonus: Drawings will vary.

WEEK 2-C (page 107)

clever — to go from place to place
roam — people, animals, or things that belong to a group
members — smart and skillful

Sentences will vary.

Bonus: A group of wolves that live and hunt together is called a *pack*.

WEEK 3-B (page 109)
1. adapt **2.** complain **3.** sly
Bonus: Answers will vary.

WEEK 3-C (page 110)

adapt — clever in a sneaky way
complain — to change to fit into a different situation
sly — to say you are angry or unhappy about something

Sentences will vary.

Bonus: Yes, red foxes can survive in the icy Arctic.

WEEK 4, Assessment (page 112)
1. clever: smart and skillful
 pounce: to jump on something suddenly
2. Sentences will vary.

Bonus: Yes, wolves live in packs with male and female leaders.

WEEK 1-B (page 115)
1. climate **2.** spine **3.** bulging
Bonus: Drawings will vary.

WEEK 1-C (page 116)

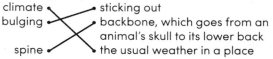

climate — sticking out
bulging — backbone, which goes from an animal's skull to its lower back
spine — the usual weather in a place

Sentences will vary.

Bonus: Chameleons can be found in both deserts and jungles.

WEEK 2-B (page 118)
1. startling **2.** bold **3.** risk
Bonus: Drawings will vary.

WEEK 2-C (page 119)

startling — causing surprise or shock
bold — to take a chance
risk — brave; fearless

Sentences will vary.

Bonus: Yes, most snakes are harmless, but rattlesnakes can be dangerous.

WEEK 3, Assessment (page 121)
1. bold: brave; fearless
 climate: the usual weather in a place
2. Sentences will vary.

Bonus: Yes, chameleons can look in two different directions at the same time.

Notes

Notes